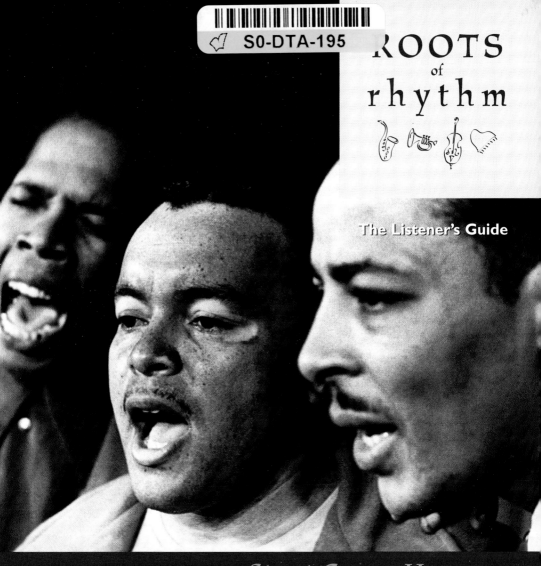

ROOTS
of
rhythm

The Listener's Guide

Street Corner Harmony

Street Corner Harmony

The 1950s saw an explosion of innovative R&B vocal groups that only later were classified under the label doo-wop—a reference to the scat-style singing common in the music. Because it is so distinctive, doo-wop tends to be admired in a nostalgic vacuum—treated like a mutant offshoot of modern music rather than an integral member of the family tree. But as this volume demonstrates, doo-wop grew directly from gospel, jazz and the blues, and it paved the way for the music of the '60s. Its innocent ballads of first love fueled the teen revolution that made rock possible. Marvin Gaye and Wilson Pickett were just two of many soul stars who got their start wailing in doo-wop groups; indeed, the genre's greatest legacy lies not in its continued popularity on oldies radio, but in the doors it opened for hundreds of talented artists.

The Listener's Guide: What the Symbols Mean

Infusions
The musician's influences and inspiration

The Sound
Style, structure and subtleties explained

Music Maker
The musician's life—the good times and the hardships

Time & Place
Circumstances and events that shaped the music

Table of Contents

Gee
The Crows 2

Blue Moon
The Marcels 4

Devil or Angel
The Clovers 6

Tears on My Pillow
Little Anthony and the Imperials 8

When You Dance
The Turbans 10

Get a Job
The Silhouettes 12

Daddy's Home
Shep and the Limelites 14

Maybe
The Chantels 16

Little Darlin'
The Gladiolas 18

Tear Drops
Lee Andrews and the Hearts 20

My True Story
The Jive Five 22

At My Front Door (Crazy Little Mama Song)
The El Dorados 24

Story Untold
The Nutmegs 26

Crying in the Chapel
The Orioles 28

"...'Gee' just took everything by storm."

—Jimmy Keyes of the Chords

Gee

Doo-wop

The Crows

At first listen, "Gee" appears to be not much more than variations on its title. "Gee....Well, oh gee...M oh gee." But "Gee" isn't a bad way to express the inexpressible—and in this case the inexpressible is that old feeling of head-over-heels love. Put to a bea that's half R&B and half Latin, the song is downrigh irresistible. It reached No. 2 on the R&B chart in th spring of 1954 and No. 14 on the pop chart—a stunning performance for an R&B vocal group. It's viewed to this day as an important "breakthrough" record for both R&B and rock 'n' roll.

Backup Blues

The Crows formed in New York's Harlem in 1951, later signing with Rama Records. At first, lead singer Sonny Norton, baritone Bill Davis, tenor Harold Major, tenor/guitarist Mark Jackson and bass singer Gerald Hamilton seemed fated to be a backup group. They backed Fat Man Humphries on "I Can't Get Started with You" and Viola Watkins on "Seven Lonely Days." But the latter was recorded at the session for "Gee," and Rama was so pleased that they released "Seven Lonely Days" with the Crows' name featured.

From "Gee" to "Sh-Boom"

Some call the Crows' (below) "Gee" the first rock 'n' roll record; others say it was "Sh-Boom" by the Chords, which was released the very same year (1954). Actually, in a sense, these two records are the same. "We patterned 'Sh-Boom'

directly after 'Gee,'" said the late Jimmy Keyes of the Chords. "We said, hey, we ought to do something like that and maybe we can have the kind of crossover hit that 'Gee' had been."

Broken Record

"Gee" was threatening to remain a strictly regional, Northeast hit until influential Los Angeles deejay Dick "Huggy Boy" Hugg (below) had a fight with his girlfriend in the studio one night in 1954 and she walked out. He knew she liked "Gee," though he was personally indifferent to

it, so a few minutes after she left he played it. Then he played it again. And again. "I'm not taking it off until you come back," he announced. A half hour of "Gees" later, she relented and called him. It was through that high-octane exposure, legend has it, that "Gee" got its foothold in Los Angeles. As for the girl, Nila, she became Hugg's wife. Well, his first wife.

Quick Hit

"Gee" was written by Crows baritone Bill Davis, and written very quickly: "Six or seven minutes," said Davis. "We were down at my sister's house and I said to the fellas, 'Let's see if we can come up with some ideas.' I wrote the words first." Rama Records' boss George Goldner added the "uh uh uh oh-gee" in the studio, where "Gee" became one of the first examples of a "head arrangement." That is, it was put together on the fly rather than plotted and charted beforehand, which makes it sound just a little bit cruder.

3

Blue Moon
Doo-wop
The Marcels

No one who has heard the Marcels sing "Blue Moon" can ever feel quite the same about this romantic old standard. It's as if a Mexican jumping bean got loose in the song and the group is just hanging on for the ride. It's not only the famous opening, but the way the exuberant background voices keep popping up right in the middle of verses—for instance, right after the word "suddenly." This rollicking take on "Blue Moon" managed to cross over with ease, spending three weeks on top of the pop chart and two weeks on top of the R&B chart in the early spring of 1961.

Zooming to the Top

EXTRA!

Colpix Records, a division of Columbia Records, wasn't on the cutting edge of R&B in '61. But A& director Stu Phillips heard a demo tape of the Marcels singing the Cadillacs' "Zoom," and he asked them to shake up a standard in a similar way. He suggested "Heart and Soul," but no one in the group knew it. They knew "Blue Moon," though, and Phillips suggested using the intro from their "Zoom" demo. They did—to the dismay of Richard Rodgers (above left), who wrote the song with Lorenz Hart (above right) in 1934 and reportedly despised this version.

♪ A Whole Lot of Nonsense

There was an informal and largely unspoken competition among doo-wop bass singers for who could create the most memorable nonsense-syllable introduction. Sherman Garnes of the Teenagers set the bar first with "Why Do Fools Fall in Love," but no one has ever created a line more memorable than Fred Johnson's "Bomp baba bomp, ba bomp ba bomp bomp, baba bomp baba bomp, a dank-a-dank-dank, a ding-a-dong-ding" in "Blue Moon" (right). Even saying it is impossible for most people who don't have double-jointed tongues—including Elvis Presley, Frank Sinatra and Billie Holiday, all of whom subsequently covered the song without the introduction. The rest of the record is nice, but the opening is the signature.

BLUE MOON

THE MARCELS

Singing the Standards

"After 'Blue Moon,' everybody wanted to be the next one to do this," said Vito Balsamo of the Salutations. "You figured it gave you a good chance for a hit." His group released an unchained rendition of "Unchained Melody," and The Marcels themselves (above) came right back with "Heartaches." It turned out to be a short trend, but a charming one.

Good Hair Day

The Marcels weren't the first group to name themselves after a hairstyle—the Poni-Tails got there first—but when they formed in 1959, they were among a relative handful of groups that were racially integrated. Richard Knauss, a white guy, started things by getting together with bass Johnson, who was black. Second tenor Gene Bricker was white, and first tenor Ron "Bingo" Mundy and lead singer Cornelius Harp were black. It was Harp, by the way, who had the marcelled hair that provided the group's name (left, top, M. Marcel, creator of the Marcel wave). But alas, the original Marcels apparently couldn't survive their success. They broke up just six months after recording "Blue Moon" in February 1961. They did, however, reunite in 1973.

Devil or Angel

Doo-wop
The Clovers

With a melody as simple as a nursery rhyme, "Devil or Angel" is a deceptively lonesome song in which the singer's love stays just out of his reach. That's the devil part. She keeps him guessing: Will she ever be his? Just as frustrating, the angel part is still in his imagination. That is to say, he has no tangible proof she's an angel. But he figures it's a pretty safe bet. "Devil or Angel" got up to No. 3 on the R&B chart in the late winter of 1956. It was one of the last hits by the Clovers, a doo-wop group that dominated the R&B charts during much of the 1950s.

Ahmet's Vision

"Yes Sir That's My Baby" was a fine imitation of the Ink Spots. Unfortunately for the Clovers, the new R&B labels that could promot them more effectively than

Rainbow weren't looking for the Ink Spots. But Ahmet Ertegun (above) of Atlantic Records liked something about the Clovers' sound, so he signed them. Atlantic was only four years old at the time and hadn't yet charted a hit by a vocal group. But Ertegun was convinced that he knew how to ge one, so when he signed them he not only directed them to change their sound but personally wrote eight of the group's first nine Atlantic singles.

6

♪ Lost Legacy

Measured by record sales, the Clovers were the most popular R&B vocal group of the early '50s. However, they haven't retained the superstar status of the likes of the Orioles and Drifters (right), perhaps because many of their later hits were pop ballads, including "Devil or Angel" (though they also did some up-tempo tunes, such as "Your Cash Ain't Nothing but Trash"). By the mid-'50s, R&B was moving toward a harder sound, so a "Devil or Angel" appeared to be on the watered-down side.

The Vee Version

"Devil or Angel" didn't fully cross over to the pop chart until Bobby Vee (below) redid it in 1961. His arrangement borrowed heavily from the Clovers' version, but Vee claimed that he hadn't heard it. His manager remembered it from black radio stations in Texas, said Vee, and thought it would be perfect for the guy who in 1961 was still working to be seen as Buddy Holly's successor. "Devil or Angel" probably neither helped nor hurt him in that quest, but it gave him another solid hit, reaching No. 6.

Rainbow Records

The Clovers formed in 1946 at Armstrong High School in Washington, D.C. They patterned their style after gospel and early R&B groups, such as the Ravens and Charioteers. It would be four years before they traveled to New York and cut their first record, "Yes Sir That's My Baby," for Rainbow—which wasn't exactly the big time. Rainbow was so low-budget that its office was a Hell's Kitchen storefront it shared with Sonny's Deli. But for baritone Harold Lucas, lead singer John "Buddy" Bailey, tenor Matthew McQuater, bass Harold Winley and guitarist Bill Harris, it was all the showcase they needed. After four years of harmonizing, they were ready.

Tears on My Pillow

Doo-wop

Little Anthony and the Imperials

With heartbreakingly precise diction, Little Anthony Gourdine spells out each syllable of his misery in "Tears on My Pillow," starting with the fairly innocuous line "You don't remember me/But I remember you" before getting to the point: "'Twas not so long ago/ You broke my heart in two." Seldom has a young singer so painstakingly articulated his troubles in such an unvarnished series of brief, direct phrases; in the chorus, for example, he sings "Tears on my pillow/Pain in my heart." The song reached No. 2 on the R&B chart and No. 4 on the pop chart back in '58, and remains a classic.

Whatever You Say, Alan

When "Tears on My Pillow" was originally released, the record label read "Imperials" —a name dreamed up by promo man Lou Galley just before its release (the group had previously been the Chesters). When disc jockey Alan Freed (above) played it, however, he said it was by "Little Anthony and the Imperials"—which came as a surprise to many, including Anthony himself. But Freed was so powerful that End Records decided whatever Freed wanted, Freed got, and it quickly reprinted the label to read "Little Anthony and the Imperials."

Queens for a Day

he Imperials formed in their hometown of Brooklyn, but got
heir first break when they rode their bikes to Queens—in
earch of girls—and ran into a member of a group called
he Cellos, who sent them to his music man at Apollo

Records. The group's record
for Apollo, "The Fires Burn No More," was not
a hit. But it got the attention of Richard
Barrett at End Records, the mentor of the
Chantels, who arranged a session for them
with End owner George Goldner (left).
Goldner thought the session was ho-hum until
they sang "Tears on My Pillow," which he
immediately heard as a hit. But the Imperials
themselves didn't agree: In
fact, they didn't like it.

Don't Mess with Neil

The Imperials were inadvertently
responsible for
launching the career
of Neil Sedaka (right),
who started out primarily as a
riter and gave label owner George
Goldner a tune called "The Diary." When
he Imperials recorded it, Goldner told End
xecutive Richard Barrett to release it as the
ollow-up to "Tears on My Pillow." But Barrett
gnored him and put out "So Much," which
e had written. Sedaka was so annoyed that
e recorded "The Diary" himself, and it
ecame the hit that got him started.

Frankie and Anthony

♪ Little Anthony rode in on the
wave of "young voice"
singers with
his natural
sharp tenor.
In 1955, the year before Frankie
Lymon (below) and the Teenagers
launched the mini-craze for the
high tenor lead sound, Anthony was

developing the same sound. In fact,
Anthony and his group competed
against the Teenagers in a talent
show where first prize was $5. No
one kept track of who won that
one, but in the long run there was
something for everyone. The
Teenagers had the first hit record
and a burst of international fame.
Little Anthony is still making a living
with his music 45 years later.

When You Dance

Doo-wop
The Turbans

Stand still when this song is playing. Or sit still. Go ahead. Try it. Can't do it, can you? If you were strapped into your seat, your head would bob and your fingers would pop. After it goes "ho-old her tight," you'll find yourself snapping out the words with the perfect pauses between: "Oh, when...a-you...dance." Boasting one of the best uses of Latin rhythms in a doo-wop hit, "When You Dance" reached No. 3 on *Billboard*'s R&B chart in 1955. It also stayed on the pop chart for 21 weeks, climbing to No. 33. Though they stayed together for another six years, this was the only hit for the Turbans.

Philadelphia Freedom

Philadelphia was a hot spot for vocal group music in the early '50s, much of it raw, unpolished and, to hard-core collectors, unspeakably wonderful. The Turbans, while they grew up on that Philly sound, came to New York to record, so "When You Dance" is tighter and slicker than many Philadelphia records. But some of that raw abandon remains— and so does a Philadelphia trademark: a prominent bass singer. Notice how often bass parts fill the holes in the harmony: That's a Philadelphia trait. It also may not be unrelated to the fact that "When You Dance" was composed by Chet Jones— the group's bass singer (above).

KEY NOTES

Like "When You Dance," the Turbans' second hit, "Sister Sook was a B-side wh ended up being more popular on playlists than its A-side ("I'll Always Watch Over You").

The Mambo Craze

The influence of Latin music on R&B in the mid-'50s is still [n]ot fully recognized. But its [pr]esence was underscored with the [li]nes "You may do a rumba or a [ta]ngo/Mambo, calypso . . . ." While [th]e "official" dances of mid-'50s [A]merica were the classics— fox-[tr]ot, waltz—the hip dances were [C]aribbean, spread by Cuban-born [ar]tists like Machito (a jazz [in]novator) and Perez Prado (a pop [or]chestra leader). So big was the [m]ambo craze in 1954 that an [ep]isode of *The Honeymooners* was [b]uilt around Alice Kramden's [A]udrey Meadows, below) wanting [to] take mambo lessons.

Sheik Chic

Herman Gillespie, manager of the Turbans, was a big fan of Steve Gibson and the Red Caps (themselves originally known as the Toppers). When he explained to his new group, a Philadelphia quartet led by Al Banks, that they should have a name like that, baritone Charlie Williams (left) snorted. "I'd rather wear a turban than a cap," he said. Watch what you wish for, Charlie. From 1955 until they disbanded in 1961, Banks, Williams, tenor Matthew Platt and bass Chet Jones (all high school classmates from Philadelphia) often appeared onstage in turbans. At least there was never any mistaking them for any other group—although they might have been confused with solo R&B artist Chuck Willis, who was also partial to wearing turbans in the late '50s.

Keep on Dancin'

Artists sometimes redo songs with an updated element; The Dells (right), for instance, re-did their 1956 hit "Oh What a Nite" in 1969. The Turbans updated "When You Dance" in 1961, recording it with more strings and a much-muted Latin beat.

Get a Job
Doo-wop
The Silhouettes

Unemployment never sounded more spirited than on "Get a Job," the 1950's version of a protest song. Lead singer Billy Horton is getting pelted from all sides: Every morning at breakfast his wife tosses the want ads at him, demanding that he find work. He makes the rounds and is turned down every time. So he heads back home and she tells him he's lying— that he wasn't really trying. What's a poor boy to do? Let off steam with a song, a song that apparently struck a chord with America, because the Silhouettes became the first R&B group not named the Platters to have a No. 1 pop hit. They topped that chart for two weeks in the late winter of 1958—and rode the top of the R&B chart for six weeks.

Help Wanted: Must Know How to Yip
Certain songs have come to define the 1950s vocal group harmony sound in the public mind, and the contribution of "Get a Job" is as clear as "yip-yip-yip-yip-yip-yip-yip-yip-moo-moo-moo-moo-moo-moo-get-a-job-sha-na-na-na-sha-na-na-na-na." In one sense, this use of nonsense syllables evolved directly from the scat singing developed in the '20s by Louis Armstrong (right) and popularized by Ella Fitzgerald.

KEY NOTES
"Get a Job" led to several answer records; one, "Got a Job," was the debut release of the Miracles. The song's success would help launch Motown Records.

Bowzer's Band

The influence of "Get a Job" was underscored in 1969 when a group of Columbia University students formed a rock 'n' roll revival group they called Sha Na Na—after, of course, the opening lines of "Get a Job." Jon "Bowzer" Bauman was the leader of Sha Na Na (left, Bauman with mouth open), and while they had a constant turnover of personnel, their time in the spotlight far exceeded that of almost all the '50s vocal groups whose songs they sang. They even had a syndicated TV show, which ran from 1977 to 1981. Interestingly, they didn't record "Get a Job" until their fourth album, in 1973.

Flip It Over

Tenor Richard Lewis brought "Get a Job" when he joined the group. It caught the ear of Philly deejay ae Williams, who recognized the hit he needed launch his own label, Junior Records. After he corded it, it came to the attention of Al Silver at Herald Records, who cked up the distribution and convinced Dick Clark to play it. As Silver lls the story, the next morning he received orders for 300,000 copies.

Job Hunt

The Silhouettes' roots went back to 1955, when North Carolina native Horton found himself in Philadelphia and recruited three local singers to form the Gospel

ember RECORDS

HAS 1958'S FIRST AND BIGGEST SMASH!

GET A JOB

Distributors report they're standing in line to get the Biggest Smash in years!

THE SILHOUETTES #1029

Tornadoes. They loved the Lord's music, but it didn't pay the rent, so after doing their gospel shows on Sundays, they would go out the rest of the week as an R&B group called the Thunderbirds. In 1956, Horton, Edwards and baritone Earl Beal brought in Richard Lewis as tenor, and he was instrumental in convincing them to go all the way to the secular side, following the successful lead of earlier groups like the Drifters and Dominoes.

Daddy's Home
Doo-wop
Shep and the Limelites

Triumph is only a few steps ahead of weariness in "Daddy's Home," but that's enough. It's been a long trip for the singer, but like those truck drivers who finally make it home in country songs ("Six Days o' the Road"), Daddy is so happy to see the front doo' that everything he went through to get there just melts away. While the record had a classic '50s R&' sound, it actually did better on the pop chart, peaking at No. 2 there in the late spring of 1961. O' the R&B chart, it reached No. 4—the biggest hit fo' Shep and the Limelites.

Road Trip

Every group has road stories. For Shep and an ensemble with whom he sang in the late '50s, the Heartbeats, a lowlight was the night they were driving through the Cumberland Mountains and their 1947 Olds blew up en route to a show in Fairmount, West Virginia. They sold the car for $15 and bus fare, figuring receipts from the show would pay their way back to New York. But the promoter blew town with the receipts, and Shep's group might still be in Fairmount except for the aptly named El Dorados—who were also on the West Virginia bill and gave them a lift.

KEY NOTES

Limelite Clareno Bassett was originally a member of the legendary Five Sharps, whose "Stormy Weatho' is considered by many to be doo-wop's rarest and most valuable recording.

He Could Sing

James "Shep" Sheppard (above, at bottom) had a pristine tenor that typified the "adult" style of New York R&B (Frankie Lymon exemplified the "teen" style). He wasn't easy to work with, however, and his groups often changed personnel. By 1961 he and the Limelites were a trio, with Clarence Bassett and Charles Baskerville (above, middle and top). Not many people could endure Sheppard's ego. "He could make you crazy," says New York deejay and former Laddins bass singer Bobby Jay. "He wasn't always a nice man. But he certainly could sing."

Miles Ahead

The Limelites began as the Heartbeats (right), formed as the Hearts in Queens in 1954. Shep wasn't in the group, but in a rival act who challenged the Hearts in a battle of the bands. The group wasn't great, but the Hearts poached him for the lead spot. They got a record deal,

and in '56 Shep wrote a "A Thousand Miles Away," a song about a girlfriend who moved to Texas. Released as the B-side of "Oh Baby Don't," it was going nowhere until Shep's fan club organized a letter-writing campaign to deejays, who flipped the record over and discovered an R&B classic.

There's No Place Like "Home"

"Daddy's Home" was the third and final song in one of rhythm & blues' strongest trilogies. James Sheppard's song "A Thousand Miles Away" kicked off the journey in 1956, when the Heartbeats rode it to No. 5 on the R&B chart. It was such a hit that he decided to go back on the road the next year, writing "500 Miles to Go." Then he apparently got sidetracked somewhere, because while he covered that first 500 miles in a year, it took him four more years to cover the second 500, and finally announce that "Daddy's Home."

15

"We all wanted to be the Chantels."

—Beverly Lee of the Shirelles

Maybe
Doo-wop
The Chantels

Some say this is the greatest teen-sound vocal group of all time, and after listening to lead singer Arlene Smith, it's hard to imagine any record could get much better. It's less a song than a cry of pure anguish, the sound of a teenage heart shattering right there on a 45-rpm record. Part of its impact also comes from the fact that it's never resolved: At record's end, Smith can still only wail, "Maybe, maybe, maybe." It peaked at No. 2 on the R&B chart in the late winter of 1958– kept from the top by "Get a Job" and "Sweet Little Sixteen," which aren't half-bad records themselves.

You Go, Girls!

It was unthinkable for five Catholic schoolgirls to sing on street corners, so their exposure was limited to formal talent shows. Then there was the problem of how to send these young women out on the road, where they would be riding buses with often older and, umm, dangerous, exotic guys in other acts. "Some of our parents just said we couldn't go," said Smith. "But that was the way you promoted your career in those days, on those tours." So a compromise was worked out: When they went, a chaperone went along.

Sorority Seniors

Many of the female groups that followed the Chantels all speak of both the group and "Maybe" with awe. Says Beverly Lee of the Shirelles (below; Lee seated bottom left):

"They were the ones who paved the way for us and the Ronettes and all the other groups that came along later. When we met them, we were in awe. But they couldn't have been nicer. They sort of took us under their wings and helped us learn how to get along when we were going on the road after we had our own first hit."

Sacred Start

A year before they recorded "Maybe," the Chantels were singing Gregorian chant (Gregorian chanters, above). Lead singer Smith and the others who would go on to form the original lineup—Lois Harris, Sonia Goring, Jackie Landry and Rene Minus—were between 7 and 10 when they met at St. Anthony of Padua school in the Bronx. They were all in the choir when they learned Gregorian chant, which requires complex vocal interplay, so they'd honing their skills for years before recording as the Chantels. When they started singing secular music, many of their rehearsals were held in the girls' locker room.

No Novelty

The Chantels are often called prototypes of the "girl group" sound, but lead singer Arlene Smith (left) cringes slightly at the phrase. "I know what people mean when they say it," she says. "But I think it held us back in some ways, and I think it's definitely hurt the perception of us over the years. It suggested we weren't serious musicians, but this cute little novelty act." They were nothing of the sort, as classics such as "Maybe," "He's Gone" and "Every Night" beautifully prove.

Little Darlin'
Doo-wop
The Gladiolas

You hear the opening notes of "Little Darlin'," that high voice singing "yi-yi-yi-yi-yi," and you just can't help wondering where that singer's going with this, and what he'll sing next. But hey, that's what the fabled "hook" in music is all about: It hooks you and pulls you in, and there's almost no way you won't keep listening. And so it has been with "Little Darlin'" for more than four decades running. It's not much more than a simple "come on, gal" song at heart, but even if the gal can resist it, listeners can't. The Gladiolas took "Little Darlin'" to the No. 11 spot on the R&B chart and No. 41 on the pop chart in the spring of 1957.

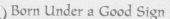

Born Under a Good Sign

The Gladiolas would later record "Stay" as the Zodiacs and have a much bigger hit with it. The name change happened when they changed record labels: Ernie Young of Excello, on which they cut "Little Darlin'," told them when they left that he owned the name. So one day while they were in West Virginia waiting for their car to be repaired, their manager Harry Gains was thumbing through a newspaper when he saw an ad for a new foreign car called the Zodiac (right). That was the end of the Gladiolas and the beginning of the Zodiacs.

Nashville or Bust

Maurice Williams (below), lead singer of the Gladiolas, had a penchant for West Indian and Latin rhythms that was never better showcased than on "Little Darlin'," which was one of the two songs with which he nagged a recording contract for

the group after they made their way to Nashville to convince Excello Records owner Ernie Young to give them a shot. Young's only condition? That they change their name from the Royal Charms—in honor of their favorites the Five Royales and the Charms—and become the Gladiolas.

The Diamonds Were Forever

Cover records are almost universally reviled in the rhythm & blues biz. But there are always exceptions, and one is the Diamonds' cover of "Little Darlin'." The Diamonds (below) were a Canadian group that had recorded a number of unremarkable covers, such as "Why Do Fools Fall in Love?" and "Ka Ding Dong." But for some reason everything clicked on their version of "Little Darlin'." It

has style and energy, and if much of the arrangement is lifted from the Gladiolas, at least in this case the Diamonds give it equal spark. "The Gladiolas' version is very good," says New York deejay Bobby Jay. "But the Diamonds' is one of the very very few that is actually better than the original."

Deejays Flipped

Although Latin rhythms were quite the rage all over popular music in 1957—a year when even typically middle-of-the-road crooners like Paul Anka spiced up their tunes with the Latin beat (his "Diana" was a smash that year)— neither the Gladiolas nor Excello Records thought "Little Darlin'" was the hit side of the record. The ballad "Sweetheart Please Don't Go" was the A-side, with "Little Darlin'" on the flip. Deejays, whose opinions no one in the music biz would dispute, soon corrected that miscalculation. In truth, Williams, tenor Earl Gainey, tenor William Massey, baritone Willie Jones and bass Norman Wade didn't mind which side got played.

Tear Drops
Doo-wop
Lee Andrews and the Hearts

Teardrops have been a bedrock of heartbroken love songs since the beginning, which may be why lead singer Lee Andrews supplements his otherwise standard plea to his lost love with the philosophical observation that he's going to need divine intervention—specifically, the biblical trinity of "faith, hope and charity"—before things get better. Whether Lee Andrews got the girl or not, his wish for a hit record was granted. "Tear Drops" hit No. 4 on the R&B chart in the winter of 1958, and even got up to No. 20 on the pop side.

WHAT You Say?

The Hearts formed at Bertran High School in Philadelphia in 1952, and in addition to Andrews included tenors Royalton "Roy" Calhoun and Thomas "Butch" Curry, baritone Jimmy McCalister and bass John Young. By 1954 they had gone to radio station WHAT to audition for deejay Kae Williams, who offered to manage them. "Maybe You'll Be There" was their first single, but they were pushed off the chart by the Orioles, who released a smoother, more polished version that got most of the radio play.

"Lee Andrews and the Hearts
excelled at smooth ballads."

—Mick Huggins

One of Those Nights

Like most of their peers, the Hearts often had trouble collecting money on live dates. One night in 1956 at Cards Beach, Maryland, they assigned roadie Bill Scott to collect their pay. After the show, unfortunately, he was

nowhere in sight. The group mounted a search for him, finally finding him in the bathroom, passed out drunk with a cigar in his mouth and not a nickel in his pocket. "Some nights," said the late Zeke Carey of the Flamingos (above, Carey front right), "were just writeoffs. And there was nothing you could do about it."

Craving for Crooners

In contrast to some black groups of the late '50s, the Hearts had a very "pop" sound, reflecting the influence of Lee Andrews' personal taste. While the other Hearts favored R&B groups such as the Moonglows and Drifters, Andrews (right) loved Bing Crosby and Nat "King" Cole, after whom he patterned his own vocal style. What makes it more intriguing is that Andrews, like many '50s R&B singers, came from the church. His father, Beechie Thompson, sang for years with gospel's Dixie Hummingbirds. But little Arthur Lee Andrew Thompson was drawn to the solo vocalists, even when he began singing with his own group and changed his name to Lee Andrews.

Bottle Brush-Off

The Hearts were one of the few groups to escape a legendary ritual at Baltimore's Royal Theater—the audience throwing miniature whiskey bottles whether they liked the act or not. If they weren't lethal, they at least distracted, so to get around the problem the Hearts came up with an up-tempo opener called "Glad to Be Here." It was so fast that the group spent the whole song in motion, thus dodging bottles. The rowdy crowd were so impressed with this strategy that they held their bottles during the Hearts' set, saving them for the Teenagers and the El Dorados.

21

My True Story

Doo-wop

The Jive Five

"My True Story" is one of R&B's most compelling melodramas, albeit one of the more puzzling. Almost 40 years later, it's still not completely clear what's happening to whom. Who exactly is crying? But no matter, really. Like opera, you don't have to understand the story to appreciate the passion in Eugene Pitt's voice. That's why "My True Story" spent two weeks at No. 1 on the R&B chart in the summer of 1961, and climbed as high as No. 3 on the pop chart.

Divide and Conquer

Some father with a family of 14 kids might divide them into a couple of basketball teams. Instead, Eugene Pitt's (above) father divided the Pitt children into two gospel choirs, which is where Eugene got his start singing. He recalls that his father would drill the two groups like sports teams, encouraging them to compete against each other. Moreover, he feels that the method served him well in his secular career. He met the members of all his R&B groups through the Battle of the Bands competitions that popped up all over Brooklyn in the '50s. As this background might suggest, Pitt himself readily agrees he was a bit of a musical hustler—and not always entirely for the causes of the Lord. "You sang for two reasons," he said. "You loved to do it and it was a good way to meet girls."

That's the Truth

Eugene Pitt says that "My True Story" *is* a true story—not his own, but that of a woman he knew from Brooklyn's Cooper projects, which was where the Top Notes formed in 1954, across from Greenpoint Hospital (right). For confirmation, Pitt has a snapshot from 1954, showing the couple on a Brooklyn playground with their arms around each other. This is "Sue" and "Earl," he says, before "Lorraine" came between them.

Deep Roots

Many R&B fans think "My True Story" sounds more like a mid-'50s song than an early '60s one, and there's a reason: lead singer Pitt had been in four mid-'50s groups before he finally got a hit. He started in the Top Notes, then moved to the Zip-Tones and the Akrons (two of his fellow Akrons vocalists included the father and uncle of the then-infant Eddie Murphy). But finally he got together with first tenor Jerome Hanna, second tenor Thurmon Prophet, baritone Richard Harris and bass Norman Johnson—all of whom, like Pitt, grew up on the early-'50s sound rather than the slicker, faster sound of the late '50s.

Slow Sequel

After waiting 20 years for someone to pick up the story of Sue, Earl and Lorraine from "My True Story," the Jive Five (below) did it themselves. In 1981 they recorded "Never Never Lie," which returns to Sue, Earl and Lorraine. They may have set some kind of record for elapsed time between original song and sequel—it's more than twice as long as the gap between Harry Chapin's 1972 hit "Taxi" and its 1980 sequel, for instance. Actually, "Never Never Lie" doesn't advance the story of the jilted lovers much. It just suggests that there's less chance someone will have to "cry, cry, whoa-whoa-whoa-whoa-whoa their blues away" if everyone is honest in the first place.

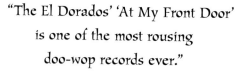

"The El Dorados' 'At My Front Door' is one of the most rousing doo-wop records ever."

—Chris Martin

At My Front Door (Crazy Little Mama Song)

Doo-wop
The El Dorados

Early R&B lyrics were filled with memorable characters, such as the Midnighters' friend Annie and the Dominoes' Dan the Sixty-Minute Man. But no list would be complete without Crazy Little Mama of "At My Front Door." Not only does she visit another man when hers isn't around, but she comes right up and knocks on the front door. The song hit No. 1 on the R&B chart and No. 17 pop in 1955—a time when such rowdy tunes scared off a lot of folks.

Credit Crunch

Lead singer Pirkle Lee Moses wrote "At My Front Door," but when it came out, it was credited to manager Johnny Moore and Ewart Abner of Vee Jay. Moses got the standard excuse: that it was easier to promote a record with a known name like Abner's on it. "I thought I was going to get paid and treated right," Moses said later, "but it didn't turn out that way."

♪ It Ain't Over Til It's Over

"At My Front Door" introduced a dilemma: the run-out ending. That is, the singing is finished several bars before the record ends, but there's still a chorus that's an integral part of the song. Most radio stations would prefer to cut off the end and go to the next record, but with "At My Front Door" the song is just plain incomplete without the da-da-da-da-da-da chorus leading up to the final "wop-wop." So most stations played it—opening the door, some say, to Simon and Garfunkel's "The Boxer" or Derek and the Dominoes' (left) "Layla."

No Pontiacs, Please

The El Dorados formed in 1952 at Englewood High School on the South Side of Chicago. Lead singer Pirkle Lee Moses, Jr., tenors Louis Bradley and Jewel Jones, baritone James Maddox and bass Richard Nickens first called themselves the Five Stars, and their biggest fan was the school's custodian, Johnny Moore, who became their manager. They wanted to name themselves after a fancy car, and since "Cadillacs" was taken, they simply used the name of the hottest Cadillac model (right).

Lefty's Gang

Doo-wop was primarily a singers' showcase (instruments were expensive), but in the studio, they were often backed by top R&B bands, as on this cut. "At My Front Door" is beautifully sung, to be sure, but an equal share of credit belongs to Lefty Bates' propulsive band. Bates was a fixture at Chicago blues and R&B sessions, and the leader of a group of superb players who could handle anything from a young vocal group to a veteran bluesman. The irresistible opening riff of "At My Front Door," brilliant in its simplicity, kicks open the door to the rock 'n' roll sound that was already creeping in. That's Al Duncan on the drums, as if you could miss him, and the sax break in the middle was played by either Cliff Davis or Red Holloway (no one remembers for certain).

25

Story Untold
Doo-wop
The Nutmegs

It's the universal cry of the teenager: No one understands me. In fact, there isn't even any point in telling anyone, because they'd never get it. But Leroy Griffin decides to go ahead and tell them anyway, with the melodrama common to all teenagers: "Well, here in my heart, there's a story untold." So Leroy explains, soaring up the scale, that since his woman left him the only thing he can do is sit around hopin' she'll come back. Having told the story, he soars even higher to repeat that yes, it's a story untold. A contradiction, maybe, but it's also the song of his life. It reached No. 2 on the R&B chart in the summer of 1955.

It Was Just a Hunch

The Nutmegs were an early favorite of Alan Freed, who played their records regularly. But when he heard in 1955 that the Nutmegs had been accused of doing "an obscene dance" at the Apollo Theatre, he took their songs off the air. Group members McNeil and Emery went to New York to clarify, explaining that they were doing the Hunch, which involved pulling the arms in and out at your side. It had a sufficiently limited lifespan that most people didn't recognize it, and Freed was satisfied with the explanation. He reinstated them on the radio and signed them up for his next package show at the Brooklyn Paramount (right).

A Cappella Kings

While the average 1950s music listener remembers the Nutmegs for solid ballads like "Story Untold" (below) and "Ship of Love," hardcore rhythm & blues fans revere the group for their unfinished work: a series of a cappella tapes they cut as demos. "The finest a cappella group I ever heard," bandleader and artist Billy Vera said of the Nutmegs. In contrast to most demos, the Nutmegs' early recordings had such varied and full harmonies that even without instrumental accompaniment, it didn't sound like anything was missing. A small-time New York entrepreneur named Irving "Slim" Rose bought those tapes around 1963 and started issuing the songs on his Times Square Records label. "Let Me Tell You" reached No. 5 on Rose's in-house sales chart, while "The Way Love Should Be" surpassed it, reaching No. 3. Rose's label even patterned its own initial doo-wop act on the Nutmegs.

Herald

45 RPM
45 RPM
Vocal Group
Time: 2:15

STORY UNTOLD
(Leroy Griffin)
THE NUTMEGS
H-452

Same Old Story

Slim Rose launched his Times Square label with a song that he took from "Story Untold." By the Timetones (right), the song was called "Here in My Heart" and began, "Well, here in my heart there's a story untold." Sound familiar? The rest of the song does take a different lyrical tack, but it shows the Nutmegs' strong influence.

Spicy Singers

One of the few vocal groups named after a spice (left), the Nutmegs' name comes from their home state of Connecticut, which is sometimes referred to as the Nutmeg State (officially, it's the Constitution State). Formed in 1954 in New Haven, Leroy Griffin was the lead, his brother Sonny the first tenor, Jimmy Tyson the second tenor, Bill Emery the baritone and Leroy McNeil the bass. Calling themselves the Lyres, they went to New York in 1954 and met the Du Droppers, who introduced them to Al Silver of Herald Records. He changed their name and chose "Story Untold" as their first release.

27

Crying in the Chapel
Doo-wop
The Orioles

Songs don't get off to a much more straightforward start than "Crying in the Chapel," which not only in lyrics but in vocal delivery is closer to a hymn than a rhythm & blues song. But since blues fans have always been torn between the devil on Saturday night and the Lord on Sunday morning, it makes perfect sense that some folks who love the former also will bow to the latter. Whatever the socio-philosophical underpinning, the Orioles hit the perfect balance on this recording; "Crying in the Chapel" was No. 1 on the R&B chart for five weeks in the fall of 1953, while climbing up to No. 11 pop. Keeping the religious spirit that year, the Orioles followed with the Top 10 "In the Mission of St. Augustine."

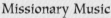 Missionary Music

While the Orioles had been known for love ballads and occasional up-tempo bluesy tunes, "Crying in the Chapel" convinced the bosses at Jubilee that the group's future lay in the Lord. Their next song, "In the Mission of St. Augustine" (the mission, right), was followed by "Robe of Calvary," "If You Believe" and "In the Chapel in the Moonlight." None was as big a hit, but at the time, R&B was under attack for being too raunchy, and it didn't hurt to be an example of God-fearing virtue. It also didn't hurt that the understated passion of Sonny Til's voice was suited to musical proverbs.

They Stayed off the Street

Only one member remains alive from the five young men who formed the Vibra-Naires in Baltimore in 1947: bass Johnny Reed, who with his friends Sonny Til (lead; below), Alexander Sharp (tenor), George Nelson (baritone, second lead) and Tommy Gaither (guitar) became the Orioles a year later. The group was a key bridge between R&B and pop vocal groups, and Reed takes pride in what the Orioles did. But there's just one thing he wants to say about a notion that often gets tacked onto their reputation. "We were never a street-corner group," he says. "That was something kids did for fun. We were professionals. We sang in clubs and shows. We weren't out on the street." So there.

King's Cross

Elvis Presley (above) loved rhythm & blues music. It's virtually impossible that growing up in Memphis, hanging out frequently on Beale Street, the 18-year-old Elvis didn't hear "Crying in the Chapel." It was all over the charts and the radio in 1953, selling 40,000 copies in 2 days (left). Any doubt was erased 12 years later when Elvis peaked at No. 3 on *Billboard*'s pop chart with his own, even more solemn version.

----That's Right! ----
40,000 IN 2 DAYS
GOING POP AND R&B

THE ORIOLES
GREATEST

CRYING IN THE CHAPEL

From Country to Blues

By 1953, the Orioles had fallen behind the groups they had helped spawn. Since their music sounded behind the times, Jubilee Records decided to take them in different direction—specifically, covering a country & western song that on the surface didn't sound much different from a hundred other love-the-Lord country ballads. But when it was married to Sonny Til's bluesy voice, something magical happened. Among other things, the song is now generally considered to be R&B rather than country.

Credits and Acknowledgements

Picture Credits

Cover/Title & Contents/IBC: Corbis
Page 2: Showtime Archives **Page 3:** (L) Michael Ochs Archives, (C&R) Showtime Archives **Page 4:** (L) Michael Ochs Archives, (R) Culver Pictures **Page 5:** (L) Michael Ochs Archives, (C) Showtime Archives, (R) Corbis/Hulton-Deutsch Collection
Page 6: (L) Michael Ochs Archives, (R) Frank Driggs Collection (P. Randolph) **Page 7:** (L) Showtime Archives, (C) Archive Photos/Frank Driggs Collection, (R) Michael Ochs Archives
Page 8: (L&R) Michael Ochs Archives **Page 9:** (L) Michael Ochs Archives, (C) Photofest, (R) AP/Wide World Photos **Page 10:** (T) Showtime Archives, (B) Michael Ochs Archives **Page 11:** (L) Photofest, (C&R) Michael Ochs Archives **Page 12:** (T) Michael Ochs Archives, (B) NBC/Globe Photos **Page 13:** (L) Photofest, (C&R) Showtime Archives **Page 14:** (T) Showtime Archives (G. Gart), (B) Archive Photos/Frank Driggs Collection **Page 15:** (L) Archive Photos/Frank Driggs Collection, (C&R) Showtime Archives **Page 16:** Michael Ochs Archives **Page 17:** (L) Globe Photos (V. Beller), (C&R) Michael Ochs Archives **Page 18:** (T) Michael Ochs Archives, (B) Mike Constantine/Timaru, New Zealand **Page 19:** (L) Michael Ochs Archives, (C) Showtime Archives, (R) Michael Ochs Archives

Page 20: Showtime Archives **Page 21:** (L) Michael Ochs Archives, (C) Corbis (M. Everton), (R) Showtime Archives **Page 22:** (L) Showtime Archives, (R) Michael Ochs Archives **Page 23:** (L) Showtime Archives, (C) Archive Photos, (R) Michael Ochs Archives **Page 24:** (T) Michael Ochs Archives, (B) Showtime Archives **Page 25:** (L) Michael Ochs Archives, (C) Gaslight Advertising Archives, (R) Vee-Jay Records **Page 26:** (T&B) Michael Ochs Archives **Page 27:** (L) Showtime Archives, (C) Michael Ochs Archives, (R) Corbis (J. Fields) **Page 28:** (T) Michael Ochs Archives, (B) Corbis (P. Finger) **Page 29:** (L) Michael Ochs Archives, (C) Showtime Archives, (R) NBC/Globe Photos

The Publisher has made every effort to obtain the copyright holders' permission for the use of the pictures which have been supplied by the sources listed above, and undertakes to rectify any accidental omissions.